Improving your reading ~~will improve your thinking~~
*—and we all need better thinking. This book provides
some of the tools.*

> Roger von Oech
> author of *A Whack on the Side of the Head*
> and *A Kick in the Seat of the Pants*

The Guide *pulls facts out fast and I can cover more
material.*

> Carl Goldenberg
> Vice President, Merrill Lynch

*One of my pet peeves is to have to read two hundred
pages to get two pages of value. In this book each page
seemed worth a page. I would buy it for that reason
alone . . . . I also appreciate the positive tone and
style along with a holistic approach.*

> Gregg Mooney
> Engineer, CH2M Hill

*I went through this enjoyable little book so quickly
and effortlessly, I don't remember learning how to
speed read—but I obviously did. At work I can now go
rapidly through dry technical reports. And I finally
have time for recreational reading.*

> G. G. Kayten
> NASA Engineer

*This is the book I should have been given in high
school—or junior high. Not only is it easy and fast to
read, but it made me laugh. After I read it again, it's
going to sit on my desk as a reference.* Read Your
Way to the Top *should be required reading for every
student and employee in the country.*

> Audrey Burkhart
> Regional Market Support Representative,
> IBM Corporation

Time is my most valuable asset. Anything that can help save time is priceless to me. The Guide *not only saved me time, it also provided an aerobic workout for my brain. Reading is now my favorite exercise!*

Elizabeth Pohlmann
Director of Communications, Touche Ross

. . . the sucker really does increase speed.

Bradford C. Matsen
Editor, *National Fisherman*

Fresh, informative, and fun . . .

Elizabeth A. Marcoux
Manager, Trust Investments,
Boeing Company

This is not just another book on reading faster—it goes far beyond, to comprehension and organizing your thoughts, time management, stress reduction, memory, creativity, and the brain. It's even useful in thinking about how to approach day to day issues and problems. I was amazed how easily Read Your Way to the Top *adapts itself to the mind of the reader, making it particularly valuable to those people who might be intimidated by the thought of learning a new discipline. I'm anxious for my wife and kids to read it.*

Geoffrey M. Bellman
author of *The Quest for Staff Leadership*

. . . Not only does it work, it makes learning fun. I'll be recommending it to my staff.

Marian K. Svinth
Employee Development Manager,
Simpson Investment Company

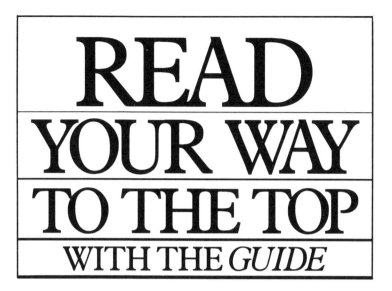

READ
YOUR WAY
TO THE TOP
WITH THE *GUIDE*

Bev —
Thanks for helping
me & my body work
my way to the top!
Read on!
Ross

READ
YOUR WAY
TO THE TOP
WITH THE *GUIDE*

Rose Saperstein and James Joseph

Illustrations by Doug Keith

A Bluechip Business Book

Bluechip Publishers
Seattle, Washington

THANKS

A heartfelt thanks to all our friends, family and colleagues for the support, ideas and spirit that helped enrich this book.

Book design by Judy Petry
Cover design by Art Attack
Editing by Bradford C. Matsen and Maureen A. Zimmerman

Bluechip Publishers
Post Office Box 31236
Seattle, Washington 98103-1236

LIBRARY OF CONGRESS CATALOGING IN PUBLICATION DATA

Saperstein, Rose, 1956-
    Read your way to the top with the guide.

    (A Bluechip business book)
    Bibliography: p.
    Includes index.
    1. Business. 2. Rapid reading. 3. Reading
comprehension. I. Joseph, James, 1954-
II. Title. III. Series.
HF5351.S34   1987   428.4'3   87-310

ISBN 0-930251-00-8 (pbk.)

Contents

How many a man has dated a new era in his life from the reading of a book? The book exists for us perchance which will explain our miracles and reveal new ones.

Thoreau

What you don't know would make a great book.

Sydney Smith

Getting Started

If we encounter a man of rare intellect, we should ask him what books he reads.

Emerson

So, here's this funny piece of plastic in your hand, and you wonder—is this for real?

It is. A visual guide, such as a finger or a pen, is the basis of several successful reading systems. The *Guide* is the basis of a new learning system that will help you stay on top of the information explosion and perform like an Einstein.

Tony Buzan, educator and author of many books on thinking skills, says in *Make the Most of Your Mind:*

> A number of studies have recently shown that use of a visual guide will increase reading speed by as much as 100 percent, while also improving comprehension, understanding, and memory. The guide focuses attention, encourages the eye to keep moving in a smooth and rhythmical fashion, and discourages the bad habits of regression, backskipping, and visual wandering.

The *Guide* is designed to do that and more. It's your trailblazer to facts not known and thoughts never pondered. It's your scholastic Wheaties.

The *Guide* is an astonishing advantage for an ambitious person. Think of all the reading you'll soon accomplish: newspapers, magazines, and business journals; poems, plays,

In the animal self-help section

Far Side cartoon reprinted courtesy Chronicle Features

and novels; textbooks, self-help books and how-to books.

Things that were once difficult will now come easily. Plunge into computers, the stock market, health and nutrition. Learn how to be a good parent or public speaker, or how to collect art or dress for success. Become an expert in your field—or learn a new one.

You'll work farther and better on the job, raising your chances for advancement and greater income. You'll manage your time better, leaving more for your family, your vacation and your daily workout. You will be, quite simply, on top of it all.

Over the next hour, the time it will take you to complete this book, you'll follow your *Guide* through dozens of practical tips and techniques that will help you to read intelligently—to grasp vital knowledge—while teaching you the foundation skills every professional should know: concentration, intuition, flexibility, relaxation, visualization, memory, note-taking, time management, experimentation, persistence, and more.

Along the way, you'll see sixteen key words listed with the chapter headings. They also occur in the text in italic boldfaced type. These are the **Guide Words** and are the essence of the book. Look at the *Guide Words* often—they're placed on the *Guide* for quick review—to help you remember the keys to reading smarter and performing better.

Throughout the book you'll find "3-Minute Breaks" that will increase your effectiveness. You'll learn why the *Guide* works, and our best guess on the gyrations the brain performs to process information quickly. If there are some questions you're contemplating, such as: "Why use the *Guide* when I can use my finger or a pen?" and "Will I have to use the *Guide* forever?," the answers, plus responses to questions never before asked, are in the back (pages 67 to 70).

Finally, you'll come to the **Guidelines**, a handy reference section (pages 74 to 83). The first part is a combined glossary/index that lists and summarizes each *Guide Word*. The second part (starting on page 79) shows you how to use the *Guide Words* as a whole-brain process for learning and achieving top performance. Try them for a project, a problem, a meeting, a homework assignment, a new business, hobby or sport. Almost anything.

As you embark on this path toward rapid reading bliss, keep the following points in mind:

- **You must practice**. Practice will make reading with the *Guide* comfortable and automatic. Practicing is easy. You know how to read. You have plenty of things to read. You can read anything to practice. Read.
- **Embrace a positive attitude**. Attitude is more important than ability. Do not think of the books and journals cluttering your desk as your opponent. Unless you are motivated, you are the true enemy; without inspiration you will not read. Come to kindly terms with your reading and turn the pages with a smile.
- **Do not set a deadline for proficiency**. Concentrate on the process of learning to read intelligently, not the product. Try not to think of reading as work. Relax and enjoy.

- **There are few absolutes**. Occasionally we will tell you to invent your own way of doing something because people, mercifully, are different and have different ways of reading. Moreover, not every technique will work for every person one hundred percent of the time. As you practice, experiment—pick what works best and modify these techniques to suit your taste. In short, develop your style. The more creative leeway you have, the more you will enjoy and profit from reading with the *Guide*. But above all, read.

Some of the techniques we introduce may seem unusual for a process as academic as reading, but bear with us. You will learn the way of the *Guide* without straining your brain or calling on complicated skills. Learning is an easy and natural process when you loosen up and engage your whole brain.

Also, please note that this book is written for the over-booked professional, reading nonfiction, with limited time. Most of these techniques can be used for pleasure reading,

Far Side cartoon reprinted courtesy Chronicle Features

but for many people that would take the pleasure out of reading. Use your discretion.

The overbooked student should also find this book indispensible; make good learning habits a goal now and you'll reap unimaginable profits for your entire life. And in today's booming market of information—massive research, changing technologies, new advances—everyone needs the inquisitive mind of a student. Education is now a life-long process and even seasoned experts maintain ongoing learning programs.

Finally, the nonreader—a person who can read but chooses not to—will find that *Read Your Way to the Top* is especially for him or her. The idea for this book was developed by a reformed nonreader who pulled himself out of an aliterate stupor through the techniques in this book. Some specific tips for nonreaders start on page 56.

So. Settle yourself in your favorite chair for an hour and wrap your mind around the notion that reading is more than just a book and a pair of eyes. The intuitive side to reading is fast, efficient and exciting.

Check Your Speed | 1

To read well, that is, to read true books in a true spirit, is a noble exercise.

Thoreau

Time yourself, in seconds, as you read the following short essay. Read as you normally would. Later, compare this to your time on the final essay. Ready...set...

The brain's gray matter, which has the consistency of liver paté, is commonly divided into left and right halves. The left hemisphere loves to process things one at a time and performs best with verbal tasks such as recognizing names; it is the analytical judge. The right hemisphere loves to process many things at once and performs best with visual tasks such as recognizing faces; it is the intuitive artist.

We use only a fraction of our brain's potential, primarily from portions of the logical left side. Western culture, particularly through schools, has concentrated more on the left brain, probably because of the ease with which verbal material can be understood, taught and tested. Right-brain activities are harder to verbalize, therefore harder to test. Unfortunately, Western society tends to ignore matter that cannot be measured.

When the brain solves a problem or achieves a task, it can go through either a left or right thought process. Great minds throughout history—Aristotle, da Vinci, Einstein, Picasso—were able to naturally link the two halves. By understanding the difference between the two modes, anyone can achieve a whole-brain approach to thinking.

Stop and check your time.

Find your approximate speed on the chart below; an average reader is between two hundred and three hundred words per minute. Jot it down in the box for later. If you don't want anyone to see your time, use the small box.

SPEED CHART

If your seconds were	Your speed in words per minute is
10	1146
20	573
30	382
40	287
50	229
60	191
70	164
80	143
90	127
100	115
110	104
120	95
130	88

Break One:
The 3-Minute Coffee Break

Breaks are good. They energize and they relax. They offer a change of pace. Some have a lesson to teach. Here's a story to remember whenever you start something new:

There once was a university scholar who visited a wizard to see what the wizard could teach him. The wizard listened for a while and then offered the scholar a mug of coffee. The scholar said, "I'll take Sanka, if you have it." The wizard poured the Sanka; it reached the brim and began to overflow, startling the scholar.

The wizard responded, "Like the coffee mug, you are full of your own ideas and will take no more. To learn, you must first empty your mug."

You've picked up this book to learn a new way to an old craft. Empty your mind of the old ways, then try the *Guide* before you question and criticize. Achievers remain achievers by experimenting and accepting new knowledge—by keeping their mugs empty. On to the *Guide*.

Use the Guide | 2

The man who does not read good books has no advantage over the man who can't read them.

Mark Twain

Hold the **Guide** like a pen or pencil. Point the *Guide* just below this sentence; move your hand, left to right, reading each sentence as the *Guide* points to it.

Keep a pace just faster than you think you can read. Don't stop or look back—keep going, keep looking ahead, keep your mind focused on your reading.

That's it. We told you it was a snap. If reading becomes a burden or your mind begins to wander, review the *Guide Words* on the *Guide*; if you forget a word, look it up in the **Guidelines**. A few seconds is all it takes.

If you're reading *Read Your Way to the Top* without a *Guide*, you may substitute your finger or any serviceable pointer (pen, letter opener, chopstick, etc.), but nothing beats the *Guide*. More about that on page 68.

There is no one right way to hold the *Guide*. As with many things, there is no wrong way either. Experiment and do what is most comfortable, which includes alternating between methods. Develop your style.

For example, try pinching the head of the *Guide* with your thumb, index, and middle fingers to produce a pivoting or twirling motion. Or try our favorite method, illustrated on the next page.

Holding the *Guide* like a pen, slide the shaft through your index and middle fingers until your fingers are at the

head. The *Guide* should sit like a cigarette in the fingers of a Hollywood starlet. By gently opening and closing your hand, you can sweep the *Guide* back and forth across the page with only a slight movement of your arm.

The *Guide* is not to be used as a straight edge drawn vertically down a page exposing text line by line. That technique looses rhythm and focus, as well as the peripheral view of subsequent lines.

Use your *Guide* for the rest of this book—and for that endless current of copy streaming across your desk. Remember to read through swiftly without stopping to reread sections; however, you may want to put a quick mark next to those sections you think you have missed, to read over later (stick-on notes work well if it's not your book).

Develop Your Peripheral Vision | 3

That is a good book that is opened with expectation and closed with profit.

Alcott, *Table Talk*

My early and invincible love of reading, I would not trade for the treasures of India.

Gibbon

Your brain may have the consistency of liver paté, but with the help of peripheral vision it can do the complex trick of interpreting an entire scene at once.

Stop reading for a moment and look straight ahead. How far can you see around you? Even though you're looking at a particular point or object, your field of vision includes a much broader area composed of many objects.

Objects, including words, have more meaning when viewed together. Think of a word as a musical note in a song. It is the combination of notes into chords and measures, not the single notes, that makes the melody.

You naturally use peripheral vision in just about every activity except reading (and thumb wrestling), so don't think you don't know how. By pushing yourself to read faster with the *Guide*, your eyes *flow* over the page, engaging your peripheral vision; this enables you to grasp groups of words, not just single words, each time you fix your eyes upon the text. You gain speed. It's like visual four-wheel drive. Vrooomm.

NARROW FOCUS

EXPANDED FOCUS

Each group of words is processed by the brain as a single thought. And because the words are viewed in context, you retain them more accurately than if you processed the words individually. Aha! This is one reason comprehension actually increases when you read faster.

Your *Guide* is the key to peripheral vision, but here are some more ways to help you stretch your reading range.

Look at any word in the middle of this page. Notice how many words you see around it. Alternately tense and relax your eye muscles while focusing on the word. When you tense, concentrate hard as if staring; when you relax, gaze softly at the word.

Notice the limited vision with the hard focus; feel the strain. Observe how many more words you see with the soft focus.

Work on expanding your focus around the point of the *Guide* as you read. Relax the focus of your eyes, develop a steady and continuous rhythm, and let your eyes flow, taking in as many words as you can. Your eyeballs should move, but your head should remain still. The magic word is "relax." See the technique on soft focus on page 55 for a variation on this.

A good way to give
your peripheral
vision a workout is
to read down the
center line of a nar-
row column of text.
Newspaper and
magazine columns
are perfect for this.

And try this exercise. Sit in a public place and observe human behavior. Look straight ahead and not out of the corner of your eyes. Although you may see a blurred image, particularly at the outer edges of your field of vision, you can sense what is there. This sensing process, similar to recognizing a blurred road sign at a distance, is a valuble tool for pulling in information.

Remember: Use the Guide

4

Guide Words: PRACTICE CONCENTRATE

If you wish to be a good reader, read.

Epicetus

Read the best books first, or you may not have a chance to read them at all.

Thoreau

Do you remember Pavlov's dogs? Whenever they heard the bell they salivated. As you ***practice***, you'll associate your new reading ability with the *Guide*. Eventually, with your *Guide* in hand, rapid reading will become automatic, like salivating at the sound of the bell. Woof.

As you practice, **concentrate** on your reading and on moving your eyes forward. Backskipping is a big waste of time. Words or phrases that you think you missed have actually been subconsciously recognized. We'll illustrate this.

Reading material abounds in extraneous and repetitive matter. These missing parts are filled in by the brain because only certain replacements make sense. Fr xmpl, y r nw rdng wrds wth mssng vwls. Now, ocasonal ettrs ae abset. It works with occasional ... missing or even if complete parts of sentences are missing. A thorough discussion of this can be found in *The Brain Book* by Peter Russell.

***Remember: Use the* Guide**. *Pick up your speed a bit. Concentrate. Do not look back.*

Mr. Russell points out that proofreading is so difficult

because "we read what we expert to read, and the faster, more expect reader will probably have corrected the errors in this sentence without realizing it." If you missed that play on letters, you're reading at the right speed. Fight the temptation to reread this passage now; that's a habit you're trying to break. Reread it only after you've finished the whole book.

Are you still moving your Guide? *Remember, keep a pace just faster than you think you can read. You have the fastest* Guide *in town.*

Impressive things happen as you increase your speed. Since the average brain processes about 1,200 words per minute, you can think faster than you can read. If you read slowly, you give your mind the opportunity to wander and to think about other things (chocolate, romance . . . the usual stuff). That is why slow readers find reading boring.

Increase your reading speed and you increase your concentration. Increase your concentration and you increase your comprehension and enjoyment. You read it here first.

Remember: Use the Guide. *Strive to achieve a rhythm as you read line after line of text with just a sweep of the* Guide, *but don't strain. Your time is precious.*

Break Two:
The 3-Minute Mental Image

This visual interlude will help you become aware of the differences between the left and right brain. Each half of the brain plays an important role in the reading process.

Make a mental image of the **L** and **R** in the following illustrations. Compare the two shapes and become conscious of their differences. When you think of the **Left** brain, always picture the block **L** made of bricks. All the lines are Linear, like the Left brain. The **L** could stand for Law, which will remind you of the judge sitting on top of the **L**. That will remind you of the judgmental **Left** brain.

When you think of the **R**ight brain, see the crafty and imaginative **R** being painted by the artist. Artist could remind you of **R**-tist, which will remind you of the **R**-tistic **R**ight brain.

Did you get all that? Don't strain to remember it. Relax, review it once after you finish the book and again next week, then you'll never forget which side of your brain does what.

The *Guide* helps your artist and judge work together when you read, but more about that later. Back to the *Guide*.

Preview Before You Read | 5

Guide Words:
PREVIEW
AIM

Some books are to be tasted, others to be swallowed, and some few to be chewed and digested.

Francis Bacon

There are books of which the backs and covers are by far the best parts.

Dickens

Reading more words per minute is important, but that alone will result in neither your fastest reading speed nor your highest comprehension. You'll perform best when you have a purpose and know what to expect. Life's like that.

Previewing provides an overview before you begin reading. It will clarify your mission and create interest. It is an excellent routine to engage your brain and prepare it for action—or inaction.

First, get to know your book. Quickly read the cover and the before and after material: copyright page, table of contents, introduction, acknowledgements, preface, foreword, summary, appendix, glossary, bibliography and index.

Is the book old, new or a classic? What is the author's intent and purpose in writing the book? How will the writer approach the subject? What is the author's claim to authority? What are the author's sources? Is the book exciting or dull? Spend just enough time to get a feel for the book—to see

what's there for you.

Next, place your thumb along the outside edge and slowly *flip* through the pages. Stop whenever anything catches your eye. Get a feel for the layout of the book. Look at the pictures, graphs, quotes, etc. Do some sample reading, or look up something specific in the index and read that. Get a feel for the writer's style and content.

Then, ask the *Guiding Question:* **Why am I reading this?**

When reading, particularly nonfiction, people often neglect to think why they're reading. Their minds wander, becoming easily distracted. When actions have no clear purpose, they're seldom carried out effectively.

Don't say that someone told you to read something. That's the worst possible excuse and will destroy every positive incentive you have mustered up until now.

Be sincere. To concentrate on reading you need both a tangible purpose and an expected outcome. Your mind needs clues to **aim** toward a goal, and it needs incentives to stay on that goal.

When your mind identifies a purpose, it will instinctively grasp what is important and skim over the rest (the same way, for example, you can hear your name mentioned across the room at a noisy party). The words you miss are subconsciously seen (or heard) and deemed unimportant. That's another reason it's not necessary to reread words you think you have missed. Comprehension does not decrease with higher speeds. It improves.

Ask the *Guiding Question: **Why am I reading this?*** all the time, especially before you commit yourself to a new book and whenever you find your mind wandering as you read. If during your reading you realize that you have no purpose, stop reading and skip ahead until there is relevant material. If you decide that a chapter or a whole book is superfluous, don't read it. Not reading something is an important rapid reading technique, often overlooked, that can save a lot of time.

Repeat the *Guiding Question* until it is a habit, and you will begin to trust your subconscious to seize the essential and reject the unimportant.

***Remember: Use the* Guide.**

Next, *hyperscan* the material. Hyperscanning is a technique that is not reading per se, but an overview of the material. It is part of previewing and an excellent warm-up to help you achieve your highest possible reading speed.

To practice, pick any book (preferably hardback, since the pages lie flatter than those of a paperback). Holding the *Guide*, try making sweeps over the page in the patterns on the facing page.

Practice until you find a pattern that's comfortable. Make up your own. The important thing is that your eyes follow the *Guide* over the entire page of print. Be sure to cover the whole page, even the last line. Spend three to seven seconds per page, depending on the level of difficulty of the material. If the book has columns, treat each column as a page.

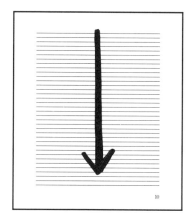 

As you hyperscan, concentrate on the page but don't read individual words. Keep your focus as soft (pages 22 and 23) as possible. Take in the big picture. Relax and don't try to remember what you see, but feel yourself comprehending the material.

A 200-page book can be hyperscanned in fifteen to thirty minutes. If you find that too tedious, try some variations. For example, hyperscan for five or ten minutes, read awhile, then hyperscan. Or hyperscan the first and last chapters, plus the first and last page of every chapter, and flip through everything else. At a minimum, hyperscan the chapters you expect to read during that sitting.

Take a moment now to hyperscan the book you've chosen. Practice each sweeping pattern, choose the method that's most comfortable, and then continue hyperscanning for another minute. Okay, go ahead.

How did you do? Let's see. Close your eyes, relax and take a deep breath. Reflect on all those pages. What words, phrases, ideas or feelings can you remember? Make a list. Speed search your brain's VCR in reverse to review what you just saw. Recalling five to ten items is a good start. Don't try too hard or it won't come—like trying to remember something "on the tip of your tongue." An Eastern philosopher might say "try without trying."

Typically, hyperscanning will produce memories of things that stand out, such as headings, boldfaced words, italicized words and words that have special meaning or associations for you. If you're hungry, words like "pizza" and "ice cream" may jump out at you. But most important, words relating to your specific purpose for reading the book will stand out.

If you can't recall specific words, what types of things were covered? The more you practice this drill the better your recall. In our reading classes it is not uncommon to find people who can recall an entire story line as well as the specifics at this speed. Anything is possible to a willing mind.

Hyperscan new books before you read them. Hyperscan all that you plan to read in one sitting. Hyperscan magazines and newspapers before you start; it's helpful in gauging how much time to allot to each article. Hyperscan your junk mail, hyperscan cereal boxes, hyperscan to read faster.

Hyperscanning is one of the most useful techniques for controlling the information explosion. Don't be intimidated by the monthly pile of journals and papers you must read to stay current in your field—you can filter the valuable information by hyperscanning.

Finally, choose your strategy. You've investigated the text, flipped the pages, answered the *Guiding Question: Why am I reading this?*, and hyperscanned. Now you're ready to pick your approach.

This is a key step. Many people lose concentration because they approach everything they read in the same way: word-by-word and page-by-page. That's okay when you read for pleasure, but not okay when time is critical and limited.

To help you choose your strategy, ask yourself: How technical or important is the material? Do I need to read the whole book or can I look up and hyperscan for specific information? Should I slow down or just skim it? Am I reading this for details or general concepts? Am I reading this for fun or profit? What will I do with the information once I read it? Should I find a better book on the subject? Identify what you need to know and decide the best way to get it. Strategies are given in Chapters 6 and 12.

Remember: Use the **Guide.**

We know, this preview business can take a lot of time. It won't, once you get the hang of it. It will save you time, particularly if you decide not to read a book or only to read the important parts that you found during previewing. Moreover, previewing helps create the motivation for reading; it will stimulate you to ask questions and seek the answers.

Ideally, previewing should take between fifteen and thirty minutes. You will be amazed how much information you absorb in that time. Spend another fifteen to thirty minutes sample reading—with the *Guide*, of course—and you will feel like you read the entire book. Previewing books as you browse in libraries or bookstores is especially fun. You may find yourself reading several books in an afternoon.

Break Three: The 3-Minute Workout

Physical activity wakes up the brain. This exercise, called cross-crawl patterning, helps your left and right brain work together.

Begin marching in place, lifting your left arm as your right knee comes up and vice versa. By lifting opposite legs and arms together you engage both brain hemispheres at once. Continue marching in place for two minutes, then spend one minute stretching by extending opposite limbs sideways (i.e., balancing on your left leg, extend your left arm and right leg).

This is a good break to take whenever you're feeling stiff or sluggish. If you're doing this at home, you don't have to remain in place. If you're doing this in the office, leave the drum at home.

"SOUNDS LIKE THE PRESIDENT IS READING AGAIN."

Be Flexible | 6
Guide Word: SENSE

I have good reason to be content, for thank God I can read and perhaps understand Shakespeare to his depths.

John Keats

To be a master reader, you must constantly evaluate what you're reading. Then, vary your reading speed and technique as the difficulty, importance and redundancy of the material changes. Practice this and you will begin to get a feel for what you are reading; once you can **sense** the content—when you can read "on a roll"—speed and technique will adjust automatically.

Perhaps you've experienced that feeling of being "on a roll." It's a time when you perform miraculously, completely lost in your involvement. Time may appear to slow down. You look back and say, "Wow, did I do that?" Author Timothy Gallwey refers to this top performance as a "breakthrough" and describes it in his book, *Inner Skiing*: "The thinking mind is in a state of rest; awareness is at a peak. For a time, self-imposed limitations are forgotten. . . ." *Read Your Way to the Top* will help you achieve this intuitive state of mind when reading.

The brain of a seasoned reader works like this: as you read, the analytical mind is comparing what you are now reading to what it read moments before. The intuitive mind and peripheral vision work together to sense what is just ahead. If the material is repetitive, the eyes pick up speed, soften their focus and search for new key material that will signal the brain to slow down.

Remember, there are no absolutes. If you encounter a key paragraph, slow down. If the material is difficult, read it word-by-word. If a paragraph is redundant, skim right over it. If most or all of the material becomes superfluous, hyperscan until you find something important.

If you slow down to a word-by-word pace, particularly for more than a paragraph, be sure to return to supersonic speed. Once you slow down, it's easy to forget everything you've ever learned about speed reading.

When you find yourself reading word-by-word, continue using the *Guide*; it will prevent you from rereading words and remind you to resume high-speed techniques.

If you don't understand a passage, read it over, but preferably at a later time. In fact, when faced with very difficult material, plan to read it quickly several times rather than once in a slow and choppy manner (more on that in Chapter 12). By reading a passage over, you see the material the second time in context with the entire passage, thereby improving comprehension and memory. Avoid what we call *roto-reading*, or mindless rereading of a sentence.

The more flexibility you develop in your reading, the more you will trust your eyes to grab the meat and skip the feathers. Your subconscious knows what's important. Trust it and you will automatically vary your speed and technique over the changing terrain of words and ideas. And *remember: Use the* **Guide.**

Reduce Tension and Stress | 7

Guide Words:
RELAX
BREATHE

Reading is to the mind what exercise is to the body.

Joseph Addison

No matter how intense the situation, a **relaxed** person performs better. While learning to relax in an emergency could take years of conditioning, relaxing in a more sedate setting is easy. Learning to relax before tackling a mammoth reading task will help you read faster and absorb more information.

Please note that the word "relax" as it is used here does not mean to slumber. "Relax" means you are calm but wide-awake and ready for action; your energy is centered and your mind is clear.

First, consider your surroundings. Are you in a relaxed atmosphere that will aid concentration? Take note of favorite places where you work well. Either do your reading there or choose reading nooks that have similar qualities: no distracting noise, good lighting, comfortable chairs, aesthetic surroundings, other people reading, etc.

If you are stuck reading in a disruptive atmosphere, don't fret; take it as a challenge to keep yourself focused on your reading. Eventually, after you develop your concentration, you'll be able to read anywhere.

Next, freeze for a moment, holding your body in its exact position. Notice that your shoulders may be shrugged or tense. Let them droop to the floor. Physically and mentally shift all your upper body weight and tension to your lower body. Now, imagine being suspended from above; your head is erect, light and alert.

How do you usually sit when reading? From now on, whenever you sit for a reading session, be conscious of your posture. Do you feel tension or stress anywhere?

If you sit in a poor position, the muscle strain that develops will eventually strain your reading. Try reading for a while as you slouch in your chair with your feet up on the desk and see for yourself. No good.

Sit up straight with shoulders relaxed in a comfortable chair (with a back) and with the book flat on the table. This is one of the better reading positions. For the next few weeks, practice reading in this position.

Sometimes you may even feel like standing up to read. That's fine, but get in the habit of shifting your upper body tension down to your lower body. Always feel for and correct the strain in your body position and you will soon learn to sense the difference between good and bad posture.

Are you still using the Guide? Slow down if you're having trouble. Concentrate. Ignore all distractions, including those nagging thoughts in your head and those real noises outside. If you think you missed something, read it over later.

Next, try some controlled **breathing** for a moment to help calm your mind. Pick a short word such as "stress," and

repeat it to yourself as you slowly drain the recesses of your lungs of air. Contract your diaphragm by pulling in your stomach. Release all tension. Exaggerate the motion. Try making a "haaa"sound in your throat and listen to the air escaping (this helps to regulate it). No, you do not sound like a sheep.

Choose another word, such as "life," and repeat it as you slowly fill your chest like a cup of water. Expand your diaphragm by pushing your stomach out and down. Breathe in life. Close your eyes and repeat a few times until you feel relaxed. Stress out, life in. Think of nothing but your breathing. Let all stray thoughts pass easily like clouds drifting overhead. Allow yourself to relax.

Deep breathing is one of the simplest endeavors you can do to help concentration and keep control of a situation. If the breathing we suggest here hits you as awkward, start by simply counting to yourself as you take deep belly breaths (stomach out as you inhale, stomach in as you exhale). The old remedy of counting to ten when you're mad is not a myth—it works.

Physical activity is great for reducing stress. Make exercise part of your weekly schedule if it is not already; it will help your reading (and a lot more). The relaxing effect of physical activity is easy to show. Loosen your wrist for a moment by flexing and stretching to avoid injury, then vigorously shake it for five to ten seconds. Let it drop to your side. Feel that? That's a relaxed hand.

Finally, be conscious of any rituals you go through that help you relax and put you in the mood for reading. Perhaps you like to steep a cup of tea, take a hot bubble bath, or don a comfortable hat or sweater. Great. Do them with enthusiasm. Make using the *Guide* part of your ritual.

Tension and stress reduce your ability to perform; relaxation re-energizes you for greater learning capacities. But relaxation is a learned skill that must be habitually used to be effective. If these procedures seem senseless, their purpose will become clear once you try them over several days and feel the difference. Relaxation is real. Relaxation works. Relaxation makes reading easier and working more productive.

Break Four:
The 3-Minute Brain Game

Read the sentence below and count the number of f's.

FINISHED FILES ARE THE RESULT OF
YEARS OF SCIENTIFIC STUDY COMBINED
WITH THE EXPERIENCE OF MANY YEARS

When you're done, turn the book upside down and recount them. The first time most people count three or four or five. There are six. You missed some because either you heard the "f" as a "v" or because your mind skipped the less important words like "of." The mind does not have to read each word. We told you that earlier. Back to the *Guide*.

Picture Your Success

Guide Words:
VISUALIZE
AFFIRM

You can cover a great deal of country in books.

Andrew Lang

It's not a new technique, but a new application of the old human tendency to daydream. Adults often call it fantasizing. Whatever you call it, it can be a useful tool instead of a distracting interruption.

To demonstrate this simply, let your mind wander to a beautiful scene and experience the warmth and joy. Feel the inner glow. Is there a smile on your face? If you dwell on the bad times, a sad mood will linger.

Our greatest achievements occur when we first create a mental picture of fulfilling our goal and then focus our energy on that **visualization**, allowing it to happen. Chief executives do it, Olympic athletes do it, all high achievers do it, although sometimes subconsciously. Now it's your turn.

Close your eyes or stare off at a point in the distance. Then picture and feel what life would be like if you could read *10,000 words per minute.*

Knowledge is wonderful. You love to read because it makes you an irresistible wit, the life of the party. Reading is fun because it's easy and you're the best.

You read a page with each breath. You read a book with morning coffee. You do a week's worth of reading in an hour, with energy, enthusiasm and determination. Your mind is an empty cup waiting for knowledge. Your concentration is phenomenal and you remember all you need to know. You finish everything you start with pure energy, enjoyment and

excitement. You're the envy of the office.

Do you get the idea? Everything is permissible. Make it creative and constructive; for example, associate a raise and promotion to your incredible reading abilities. Include an association with the *Guide* and you will enhance your reading performance whenever you use it.

***Remember: Use the* Guide.**

At first you don't have to make your visualization or fantasy grandiose. Start with simple, one-line ***affirmations***, positive statements worded in the present, and continue using them throughout the day, especially when you need a quick word of encouragement:

- I find reading to be relaxing and easy.
- The *Guide* makes reading fast, fun and easy.
- Each moment I read faster and comprehend what is necessary for me to know.
- The *Guide* allows me to concentrate clearly, oblivious to all distractions.
- I remember and understand what I read.
- The *Guide* instantly helps me to relax while my mind stays sharp.

- I am alert and concentrate clearly when I read.
- I read fast with the *Guide* with better comprehension, understanding, and memory.
- I enjoy reading my way through the information age.
- Speed reading with the *Guide* is a cinch and I'm the best.
- My reading potential is unlimited.
- I reach top reading performance by using the *Guide*.
- I effortlessly manage the information explosion by using the *Guide Words*.
- The *Guide Words* help me achieve my goals.
- Using the *Guide* puts me on top of it all.

Pick an area in which you need work and make up your own.

Whenever you begin a reading session, affirm and visualize to reduce stress and to put yourself in a positive frame of mind. Combine your mental exercise with your moment of controlled breathing. See and feel yourself as a master reader.

We're not suggesting you immerse yourself into a guru-meditation trance or something. Just take a couple of deep breaths and give yourself a little pep talk. That's all. It's like psyching yourself up for a sporting event; it only takes a few seconds.

Let your mind work for you even before you begin and you will be well on your way to completing the task at hand.

Retain What You Read | 9

Guide Words:
REMEMBER
BREAK

I divide all readers into two classes; those who read to remember and those who read to forget.

William Lyon Phillips

Studies have shown that we forget eighty percent of what we learn within twenty-four hours unless we reinforce the memory. Think back to what you read yesterday or last week. How many details do you recall?

We **remember** things that are meaningful and interesting. You never had trouble remembering your favorite subject in school, did you? Previewing is an excellent way to arouse interest, particularly if you find the subject dull. Previewing primes your mind to better absorb and retain information.

Strive for high comprehension; the better you understand the information, the easier it is to remember and recall. Test your comprehension by asking: What did I just learn?

Don't try to remember everything you read, just the important stuff. Ask the *Guiding Question: **Why am I reading this?*** to help you retain the vital information. If you're reading to answer questions, skim the questions every now and then. If you're doing research, skim your outline every once in a while.

Memory is also strengthened through repetition, especially if you repeat using a different learning method. Think about what you read; it's okay to stop and reflect on your reading, but not on your plans for the weekend. Take notes, which help you to think, then review them. Talk about what you read; your plants will listen. Read material twice quickly rather than once slowly (see Chapter 12); after you know what information is available, choose the details you want to remember.

Keep in mind that even if you read a book slowly, you remember only a fraction of the information—the same amount as you would if you read it through quickly—unless you reinforce the memory. So why not read quickly? You'll retain the same amount, if not more.

Humor is a terrific memory tool; people remember things that are unusual. Humor is refreshing. Harry Lorayne and Jerry Lucas, authors of *The Memory Book*, apply humor as a basic memory rule: "In order to remember any new piece of information, it must be associated to something you already know or remember *in some ridiculous way.*" Put humorous relationships into your thoughts and notes. If you have a choice, choose books written in a hu-

"OK, listen up! The cops are closing in on this place, so here's our new hideout: 455 Elm Street. ... Let's all say it together about a hundred times so there'll be no screw-ups."

Far Side cartoon reprinted courtesy Chronicle Features

morous or light style. If you have to remember vast amounts for work or school, then a memory book with mnemonics (memory aids) is a must. The three memory books in the bibliography all contain mnemonics.

Finally, take short *breaks*, like those in this book, often. Recall is greater at the beginning and at the end of a learning session. Between thirty to sixty minutes is the optimal period for studying. No matter how intense your reading or how short your time, re-energizing yourself with a few moments of deep breathing, visualizing, exercising or stretching will prevent exhaustion and improve your performance. More beginnings, more endings, better recall. Please don't abuse this but *break before burnout*.

And don't forget, *use your* **Guide.** A visual guide focuses attention, thereby improving memory.

Break Five:
The 3-Minute Visual
Vacation

As you read, tension, stress and fatigue build up, especially in the eyes. This prevents clear thinking. An excellent remedy was devised by Dr. William H. Bates, who designed palming as a method for natural vision improvement in 1918. We combine it with a visualization exercise.

The only time our eyes are at a complete rest is during total darkness. Close your eyes and cup your hands over your eyes. Try that for just a second and feel the instant relief. Do not press, but make sure no light can penetrate your fingers. Relax through breathing: exhale stress, inhale life; repeat several times. Clear your mind of all thoughts.

Picture yourself in a pleasant place and allow the serenity to fill your body. Roll your eyes around to see the entire scene. If you imagine yourself at the ocean, have your eyes follow the waves in and out. Move your eyeballs up and down, side to side, and diagonally. This helps relieve muscle tension. Give yourself some affirmations. Slowly uncup your hands and open your eyes.

Do this exercise for a few minutes whenever you feel fatigue or eye strain. Back to the *Guide*.

Take 10
Memorable
Notes

Guide Word:
MAP

*The love of books is a love which requires
neither justification, apology, nor defense.*

Langford

Note-taking will dramatically increase retention. Notes make you think about the vital information, even if you never look at the notes again.

Notes should be brief. Use a key word or two to represent the broad concepts. Make them visual and creative; include color, pictures and diagrams. Channel your artistic energy used for doodling into your notes. Take notes that are worth remembering.

Notes do not have to be written in outline form; that appearance makes a minimal impression on your memory. Try putting your ideas into two-dimensional ***maps*** like the one on the next page, which summarizes Chapter 9 on memory.

Mind maps work the way your memory does, by associating key ideas. To draw a mind map, choose a key word or phrase for the major point and place it in the center of your note paper. Then let all the supportive thoughts branch out from that center.

You may not see the beauty of mind maps right away. Experiment with two-dimensional mapping over the next few weeks; for example, do shopping lists in both maps and linear outlines and compare. Although we've done a mind map for Chapter 9 and one for the entire book in Chapter 13, they may seem confusing—because you didn't draw them. Mind maps not only reflect the unique pattern of an in-

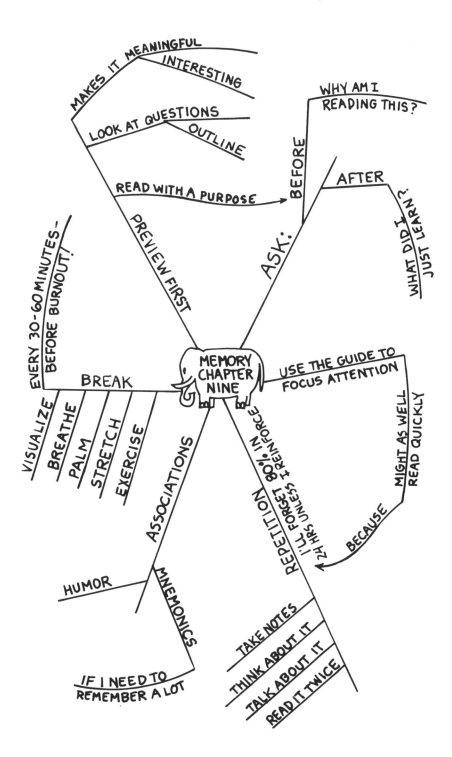

dividual's brain, the key words may only have meaning to the person drawing them.

Creating your own mind map is best and will have the greatest impact on memory. Draw mind maps for the other chapters for practice.

Take notes at the end of a reading session or after a complete thought (paragraph, subsection or chapter). This will exercise and test your memory and comprehension. It's best to reword phrases. Also, keep them neat; print the words.

There are shortcuts for taking notes: summarize ideas by making comments in the margins; underline or highlight text with a marker. These variations are faster than note-taking, but slow you down during review.

Don't make the mistake of painting the whole text with your yellow highlighter. You must underline consciously. Don't underline just to read it over before a big event (meeting, presentation, test); that only delays your thinking. Underline to reinforce ideas, to highlight the main points. Change colors or put checks or stars at points that are the most important to review. Also, it's a good idea to confine this activity to your own books.

***Remember: Use the* Guide.**

Manage Your Time

A man ought to read just as inclination leads him; for what he reads as a task will do him little good.

Samuel Johnson

If finding time to read is hard for you, then time management is essential. Managing your time is easy, much easier than wasting time. Make a daily "To Do" list. Also make monthly or yearly lists that include goals. List everything that needs to be done.

Prioritize items into three groups: "A" for the most important, "B" for the medium important, and "C" for the least important. Then assign priorities to the tasks within each group.

Consider each item on your A list and ask yourself what would happen if you didn't do it. If your life wouldn't fall apart, cross it off your list. Try to cross off two or three things. Repeat this process for the B list. Throw the C list in a drawer and forget it.

There. You just found at least one extra hour per day in which to read. Now decide what books, periodicals and other reading material you need or want to read and decide what time of day is best for you to do various types of reading. Reserve your thought-intensive work for your prime working time, i.e., don't read a *Vogue* or *Sports Illustrated* in the morning if that's when you're the freshest.

Then set aside time to read. This should be time spent only on reading and not on thinking about the cheesecake you had for lunch. ***Plan*** how much time you will spend reading, how many pages to read and when to take a break. Document this in your daily and weekly schedules. If you don't write it down, you won't do it.

Mark off the pages you intend to read. Paper clips, rubber bands and stick-on notes work well. Go easy on yourself. Only approach a realistic amount of material. If you complete your reading sooner than you thought you would, take a quick break and start on the next section. Get in the habit of completing what you set out to do and you will always be motivated to do more.

Always carry a book around with you to take advantage of unexpected free time. That's a great habit to develop. Never, but never, go to the post office without a book.

Make good use of your break time. Refresh yourself with light reading during breaks from your regular work. When you break during your reading, plan your schedule for tomorrow, and include time to read.

And make good use of your reading time: ***Use the Guide.***

Break Six:
The 3-Minute Plan

Do you know what you'll be doing two hours from now? How about tomorrow? Take three minutes now and plan.

Just as you always ask the *Guiding Question*, always ask its close cousin, "Lakein's Question: What is the best use of my time now?" (from the book, *How To Get Control Of Your Time And Your Life*, by Alan Lakein). Ask it often to help you plan your day, including time for reading.

Be realistic. Don't plan every minute of your day. Allow time for Murphy's Law to show its ugly face. When a problem arises, plan to take a minute to relax and remember your priorities. And if you never seem to find time for fun, just schedule some pleasure into your calendar.

When you find yourself procrastinating on a big project, break it up into baby projects. Make a list of the specific activities you must perform to succeed. By taking smaller steps the project will seem more approachable. Remember the saying: inch by inch it's a cinch; by the yard it's hard. Back to the *Guide*.

Play with These Techniques

12

Guide Word: EXPERIMENT

It is chiefly through books that we enjoy inter-course with superior minds.... In the best books, great men talk to us, give us their most precious thoughts, and pour their souls into ours.

William Ellery Channing

People have different interests and abilities. The following techniques are only suggestions and not everyone will find them useful. ***Experiment.***

Reading It Over

We've mentioned that it is beneficial to read something more than once. Try this: (1) Do a three to seven seconds per page hyperscan for the first reading. Mark those paragraphs or sections that require more in-depth reading (stick-on notes work well if it's not your book). (2) Then slow down to an eight to fifteen seconds per page hyperscan for the second reading. Mark any new sections you want to look at more closely; delete the marks by sections that were clarified by this reading. (3) Either do a third reading at fifteen to twenty seconds per page or just read over those sections that you marked in your first two readings. You will achieve the greatest retention of information by spacing your readings over several days.

Play with this trick: tell yourself you will do the first reading quickly to get the general idea and then go back for a second reading to gather the details. There is a good chance you'll decide not to read the book again, or you'll only need to read over certain sections.

Soft Focus

Try this technique. As you read, look at the white space between the lines. Sweeping your eyes across a blank white line is easier than fixing on words. This forces you to maintain a soft focus and read with your peripheral vision. This technique will help when you eventually read without the *Guide*. Yes, there will come a time when you may not need the *Guide*. We will discuss that sad event later.

Eliminating Bad Habits

Do you mumble when you read? Does your body twitch and shake while you read? Do you hear the words as you recall them? Those are poor habits that many people have developed. They slow you down. To stop mumbling, shaking and subvocalizing, you first must be aware that you do them. Once you bring these faults—or any bad habits—into your consciousness, you can stop them by concentrating on always correcting yourself. Using the *Guide* helps combat these habits. The *Guide* pushes you so fast that you cannot possibly say, feel or hear each word.

Learn to Love What You Hate

Here are a few tricks for the material you hate to read, that horrible stuff over which you endlessly procrastinate.

Break it up. Divide the material into bite-size pieces. Choose five, ten, or even just one page. Mark off the section and read it; reading a few pages is much easier than a whole book. It's only psychological, but it works.

If time permits, check the bibliography and find another book or article that is more readable. If the new source won't serve as a substitute, at least it will make the original source more understandable and, with some luck, more interesting.

You can further break the barriers of resistance toward reading by identifying the resistance. Ask yourself: What don't I like about this? Sometimes the reason may not be obvious and may have nothing to do with the reading material. Try to get in touch with your feelings. For example, maybe it's a splendid summer day and you don't feel like reading. Fine. Reschedule a more appropriate time for reading. But don't just say you'll read it later—that's a sure way to procrastinate; mark it in your appointment schedule.

A Shortcut That Works

Read just the first sentence of each paragraph. This sentence is usually the topic sentence. What follows is supplementary information, although sometimes the last sentence is the topic sentence (if you sense that, read both until you figure out the pattern).

Use this technique when you're tired and don't feel like reading quickly. This technique will get you rapidly through a book at your old reading rate with a good idea of the content.

Also use this technique when you are extremely pressed for time. In other words, read just the first sentence but read it at your new accelerated rate.

In both cases, keep the following points in mind: continue to use the *Guide*; let your eyes drift past the remaining sentences to scan for any key words; and continue to read intelligently, i.e., use all the other techniques you've learned.

For the Unmotivated Reader or Nonreader

First, change your attitude. Regularly review the affirmations in Chapter 8. In addition, affirm to yourself that you have all the skills necessary for reading, that you have molded those skills into a personal style that makes reading enjoyable, and that you really can become a fast and prolific reader. Say to yourself, "Reading enriches my life and is my gift to myself."

Next, take time to select—to hunt for—books that you find irresistible. Try some of the following suggestions:

- Experiment with different kinds of books—self-help, how-to, biographies, fiction, humor, etc.—and with different authors; ask booksellers, librarians and friends for recommendations.
- Check with local bookstores and the book column of your local newspaper for autograph sessions and readings

and try to attend one—the book will have more meaning after you meet the author.

- Pick a book that has an audiocassette available (most popular fiction and nonfiction today) and listen to that first; browse the audio section of your local bookstore or library for ideas.
- Pick the book version from a great movie you've seen or rent the videocassette and view that first. Many popular nonfiction titles are now available on video; look in the video section of your local bookstore or library for possibilities.
- Pick a subject area, perhaps a hobby, and start a collection of books. Don't worry if you don't read them right away—they're there for browsing, for reference, and for developing a library and a love of books.
- Select books that are easy and enjoyable; choose books that are visually appealing; and stick with hardback books because they usually have more white space between the lines, bigger type, and are easier to handle (they can be laid flat on a table, and the pages turned easily and quickly).

In addition to all the skills and techniques you've learned up until now, the following are a couple of tricks that are guaranteed to get the nonreader reading:

- As we pointed out in Chapter 9 on memory, we only remember a fraction of the material we read. Consequently, instead of reading a book cover to cover, look for something worthwhile to remember. Browse a book using a combination of flipping and hyperscanning (discussed in Chapter 5), searching for three interesting points. Once you find three bits of useful information, put the book aside. If you felt the book worthy of a closer inspection, return to it on a later day and repeat this process.
- Randomly pick any page and start reading. If after a couple of paragraphs you lose interest, flip and read until you find something interesting. Then turn back and

read the beginning of that chapter. Keep doing this until your interest is piqued enough to read the first chapter. You may end up reading the book backward, but your brain will organize the salient points. At least you read it. Good work.

Finally, a few reminders: set a reading goal and write it down, keep a written schedule of your reading and discipline yourself to follow that schedule, always carry a book and keep another couple by your bedside, and persist through all obstacles.

If you know a nonreader, lend him or her this book. By improving his reading skills, he'll take a new interest in reading. If you know someone who has limited reading ability, read this book aloud together with him. The techniques in this book are simple, fast and effective—just what he needs to give him the confidence to *read on.*

For All Readers

You may choose to do some reading, such as a novel or the Sunday paper, slowly. That's fine. Read them upside down if you like. Just be careful you don't make reading slowly a habit that carries over to reading that must be done quickly. You may even find that some of these techniques can be useful in pleasure reading. For example, you can hyperscan a novel to find your place or to refresh your memory about a character or story line.

You should now feel confident that you have a powerful tool and a variety of reading and learning strategies to use whenever necessary. If you always **remember to use your Guide** you will never be intimidated by the information age again.

Review It Over and Over | 13

Guide Word: **PERSIST**

If you cannot enjoy reading a book over and over again, there is no use in reading it at all.

Oscar Wilde

Reading through something once will barely make an imprint. It's critical that you read this book over many, many times during the next few weeks and months. ***Persistence*** in practicing and using the skills presented in this book is the only way to learn and understand these techniques, and to turn them into habits. Persistence is the key to accomplishing anything difficult. Thomas Edison said it best: "Genius is 2 percent inspiration and 98 percent perspiration."

Future readings should cover only Chapters 2 through 13 (you may skip the breaks) and should take twenty to thirty minutes. Read through swiftly without looking back; if you miss something, put a quick check mark and catch it next time. Clock yourself and try to beat your old time with each new reading.

Now, say to yourself: "Reading is fun, reading is easy, and reading is important. I am going to set aside twenty minutes a week, every week for the next ten weeks, to read this book. I'll do it Monday morning at breakfast to start the week with a positive action. Or I'll do it anytime I find myself slipping into my old reading habits. And I'll do it as often as necessary. I'll keep this book handy at all times—in my briefcase, next to my dictionary, in my car, on top of the TV or in the refrigerator—as a constant reminder.

"At the very least, whenever I have a lot of reading to do, I will take a three-minute break and study the **Guidelines** at the end of the book. That alone is enough to get me motivated.

"And at the very, very least, I will always carry my *Guide* with me just as I always carry my pen, my wallet, my house keys and, from now on, a book. I will refer to the *Guide Words* and ask the *Guiding Question:* **Why am I reading this?** whenever I find my mind wandering as I read. I will always **remember to use the Guide**."

Quickly review what you just learned with the mind map on the next page. Then take the speed test in the next chapter to see how much you've improved.

THE YOUNG THOMAS EDISON

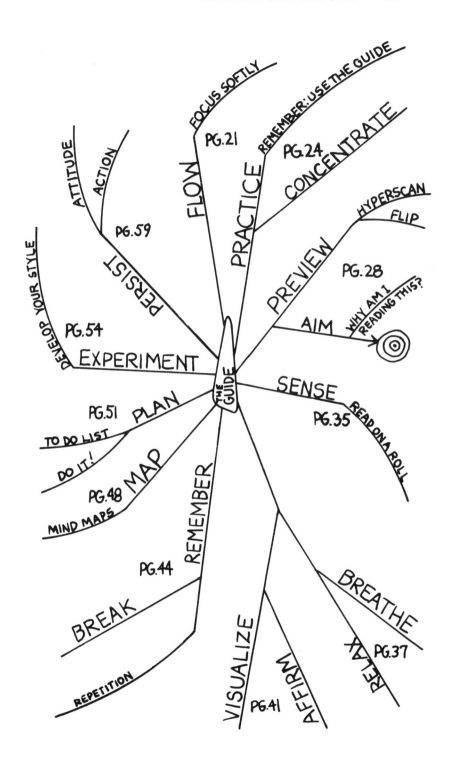

Check Your Speed Again | 14

I cannot live without books.

Thomas Jefferson

Begin timing now . . .

It is hard to pinpoint exactly where creative insights come from. They often hit when least expected—in the shower, driving, or right before bedtime. Unfortunately, they don't pop out when we need them the most, such as when we are sweating at our desk over a new proposal.

The creative process works like this. You first gather all the necessary information, then ask yourself questions that relate to the solution you are seeking. Now relax. Do something else. Let your subconscious work on it. Sleep on it.

It is a good idea to set a deadline, so your brain has some idea of when you need the solution. When the solution comes to you, oftentimes in a flash, you must then test or analyze it to be sure it works.

You can also apply the creative process to your decision making and generate answers through "gut feel." Avoid getting buried in the details of a situation; instead look at the overall picture. Also, look at unrelated subjects and seek information from unconventional sources. Then learn to listen and trust your feelings and that voice within. By following this process, anyone can develop and perfect the intuitive hunch.

Stop and check your time. Figure your reading rate with the chart on page 17 and compare it with your earlier speed.

A Final Word

I am a part of all that I have read...

John Kieran

Life being very short, and the quiet hours few, we ought to waste none of them in reading valueless books.

John Ruskin

Congratulate yourself, you're getting it. It's easy to quit when trying something new. Just ask the hundreds of thousands of people who have taken reading courses but still read with their old habits.

The motivation to continue must come from within. Understanding this will come through practice: the more you practice, the more you will achieve; the more you achieve, the more you will be motivated. Practice makes progress.

If you persist in your commitment to use the *Guide* and read intelligently, the genius in you, as well as new opportunities, will emerge.

How about a book on creativity to help you develop that million-dollar idea? Or read *Consumer Reports* and avoid the aggravations of shoddy merchandise. Or use your windfall of free time for a class on starting an import business; then use the *Guide Words* to help implement a business plan. Finally, relax with Dickens or Michener. Start now.

If you wait, you'll procrastinate. When you finish this book take a 3-minute planning break. Decide what time of day will be best to read and block out that time on your daily schedule for the week (don't forget today).

Then start reading. Even if you can only spare ten minutes, start reading now; put it off and you'll keep putting it off.

During your next 3-minute break, list in priority order the reading that you want to accomplish this month. And decide what book to carry around under your arm everywhere you go; if your time is up now, at least take hold of that book when you put this one down and stick it under your arm.

One more time: *Use your* **Guide**. And a better life is possible.

We remind you to take a moment now or at the end of the book to review the illustration on the left/right brain on pages 26 and 27 and to read again any sections you may have gone over too quickly.

A Note about the Brain

The brain is a wonderful organ; it starts the moment you get up in the morning and does not stop until you get to the office.

Robert Frost

What researchers *don't* know about the brain is vaster than what they *do* know. Like many concepts that were accepted a decade or two ago, old knowledge now misses the mark. While the techniques we offer in *Read Your Way to the Top* work, precisely how the brain performs is not clear. As new knowledge surfaces, the explanations presented here may be revised and, hopefully, new techniques developed.

Also, please note that some explanations are simplifications—for example, those we used to present the concept of the left and right brain. The brain is too complex to definitively divide into just two parts, but such a division is an easy way to begin a discussion on the brain's different modes of functioning.

Questions and Answers

How does the *Guide* work?

The following simple experiment used by Tony Buzan, educator and author, demonstrates how our eyes move with the aid of a visual guide. You'll need an assistant, so you may have to use your imagination for now and try it later with a friend.

Have her or him stand a foot or two in front of you. Now, tell her to slowly outline an imaginary two-foot-diameter circle, moving only her eyeballs. The pattern the eyes follow should look something like this.

Okay, a little crooked, but, "So what?" you ask. Next, trace the same two-foot-diameter circle with your finger and ask your partner to follow your fingertip, again moving only her eyeballs. The new pattern will look like this.

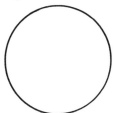

Behold how smoothly guided eyes follow. You'll notice that understanding the *Guide* does not require a degree in neuro-optics.

Mr. Buzan notes an example of "*Guide*like" behavior in an otherwise unsung group in our society, accountants. Did you ever notice accountants running their pens or pencils down a column of numbers? They do that instinctively.

Will I have to use the *Guide* forever?

Probably not. Once you train your eyes and brain to move quickly you won't need a visual guide. At that time you will probably read faster without a pointer. We have found that we go back and forth between using the *Guide* and not using it (but we always keep it nearby as a reminder). It depends on what we're reading, how we're reading it, how alert our brain is at the moment and how many distractions are present. Also, it depends on whether we're in shape: that is, whether we've recently been doing a lot of reading. Experiment and do what is most comfortable.

Why use the *Guide* when I can use my finger or a pen?

Most likely you were taught not to use your finger when you learned to read. We're not sure why, but probably you pointed at each word and that slowed you down. You should have been taught to move your finger faster and faster.

The value of having a bona fide, one hundred percent, dedicated pointer, is many-fold. However, if you find yourself stranded with only your finger in hand, by all means use it. Some sort of pointer, such as a pen, is better; however, you will find substitutes both visually distracting and harder to move across the page. This may result in weary eyes, a tired hand, sloppy technique and a return to your old habits.

Your specially designed *Guide* requires the minimum effort to hold, point and sweep across the page. The simple design is nondistracting, yet will easily draw your eyes to a point.

The *Guide* has psychological benefits, too. First, a pointer is useless if it's never used; your *Guide* is a constant reminder—like yarn tied around your finger—to push yourself to use the techniques you've just learned.

More subtle, but more powerful, the *Guide* will effortlessly trigger the positive mind-set necessary for productive reading. It will have you instantly eager over your reading, always reminding you of rapid reading bliss.

Most important, the *Guide* lists key words from the text that prompt you toward intelligent reading habits. These words represent a set of skills you can use every day in the office or classroom to help you work further and smarter.

Finally, the *Guide* can be used as a bookmark (try that with your finger). If, over time, you find you prefer your finger or a pen, continue to use the *Guide* as a bookmark. By keeping the *Guide* nearby you will still receive its psychological benefits. If you need further encouragement, just refer to your friendly list of *Guide Words*. It only takes a few seconds.

What is the difference between reading and recognition?

Reading is a verbal process. It takes place in the left brain. It is linear and sequential in nature; consequently, information is taken in piece by piece.

Recognition is a visual process. It takes place in the right brain. It is spatial and holistic in nature; consequently, information is taken in as a whole. Recognition is faster than reading; therefore, the faster you read, the more recognition you do.

How are the *Guide*, the right brain and speed reading related?

By forcing your eyes to move quickly, reading with the *Guide* accesses the high performance potential of the right brain. First, it enables you to do more and more recognition (Chapter 4 and the question preceding) so information is taken in visually as well as verbally. Second, it forces you to use your peripheral vision (Chapter 3); this allows you to absorb more information at once, letting the right brain perform at its best.

By arousing the right brain you begin to read intuitively and tap into tremendous sensing powers in several different ways: you gain a feel for the paragraph being read, which lets you adjust your speed (Chapter 6); you gain a feel for the overall book, which lets you adjust your strategy (Chapter 5); and you engage your automatic filtering system, which lets you grab key information (also Chapter 5).

Finally, *Read Your Way to the Top* looks at subtle areas not directly associated with reading, such as relaxation (Chapter 7), exercise (Chapter 7 and Break Three), visualization (Chapter 8) and attitude (Getting Started, affirmations in Chapter 8 and Chapter 13). This holistic, whole-brained approach, which can be used in all aspects of your life, balances the mind, body and spirit for top performance. Enjoy.

Read These Books

Rapid Reading

Buzan, Tony. *Make The Most Of Your Mind*. New York: Linden Press/Simon and Schuster, 1984. A great how-to book covering speed reading and effective reading, memory, listening, seeing, note-taking, creativity, numeracy and analysis.

Buzan, Tony. *Speed Reading*. New York: E.P. Dutton, 1984. Good discussions on the brain, eye movement, reading problems, skimming and scanning; many tests and drills.

Riel, Arlene. *Speed Reading Made Easy*. New York: Doubleday & Company, Inc. 1985. If you want to read another book on speed reading, then read this one.

Russel, Peter. *The Brain Book*. New York: E.P. Dutton, 1979. Check the chapter on reading; also good stuff on note-taking and memory.

Visualization

Gawain, Shakti. *Creative Visualization*. Mill Valley, CA: Whatever Publishing, 1981. Great techniques to master visualizing.

Memory

Buzan, Tony. *Use Your Perfect Memory*. New York: E.P. Dutton, 1984. Techniques for remembering just about everything.

Higbee, Kenneth L. *Your Memory: How It Works And How To Improve It*. New Jersey: Prentice Hall, 1977. The title describes it. Good blend of theory and technique.

Lorayne, Harry and Lucas, Jerry. *The Memory Book*. New York: Stein and Day, 1974. Learn the feats of memory.

Time Management

Fanning, Robbie and Tony. *Get It All Done And Still Be Human*. New York: Ballantine Books, 1979. A lively, creative approach.

Lakein, Alan. *How To Get Control Of Your Time And Your Life*. New York: Signet, 1973. By the Father of time management; a classic.

Mackenzie, R. Alec. *The Time Trap*. New York: McGraw-Hill, 1975. Geared for the business person.

Scott, Dru. *How To Put More Time In Your Life*. New York: Rawson, Wade Publishers, 1980. A more personal approach; looks at individual psychology of time use.

Creativity and Problem Solving

Adams, James L. *Conceptual Blockbusting: A Guide To Better Ideas*. New York: W.W. Norton and Co., 1979. Just as the subtitle states.

Harmon, Willis and Rheingold, Howard. *Higher Creativity: Liberating The Unconscious For Breakthrough Insights*. Los Angeles: J.P. Tarcher, 1984. Exploration into the creative process; a look at creative breakthroughs and a process for using and developing your insights.

Von Oech, Roger. *A Kick In The Seat Of The Pants*. New York: Harper and Row, 1986. The creative process creatively illustrated.

Von Oech, Roger. *A Whack On The Side Of The Head*. New York: Harper and Row, 1983. A how-to book for unlocking mental blocks.

Vision

Corbett, Margaret Darst. *Help Yourself To Better Eyesight*. New Jersey: Prentice Hall, 1979. Bates method for vision improvement. If you liked palming, this book has additional eye exercises.

Brain Books

Blakeslee, Thomas R. *The Right Brain: A New Understanding Of The Unconscious Mind And Its Creative Powers*. New York: PBJ Pub./Anchor Press, 1980. Good to get to know your other half.

Buzan, Tony. *Use Both Sides Of Your Brain*. New York: E.P. Dutton, 1983. The first book on mind maps and Buzan's organic study method.

Ostrander, Sheila and Schroeder, Lynn. *Superlearning*. New York: Dell Publishers, 1979. Techniques for powerful learning.

Guidelines

This is the glossary/index for the *Guide Words*, sixteen key words from the text that are the essence of *reading your way to the top*. And the *Guide Words* aren't just for reading—these words can be used as *guidelines* to help you through any activity. More about that on pages 79 to 83.

What's the **Guide**? It's a specially designed visual guide to help you read smarter and perform better. Comfortably holding the *Guide*, underline all text in a smooth and rhythmical fashion. Keep a pace faster than you think you can read. Do not stop, do not look back, do not let your eyes or your mind wander. If reading becomes a burden or your mind begins to wander, review the *Guide Words* on the *Guide*; if you forget a word, look it up in the **Guidelines**. If, over time, you find you prefer your finger or a pen, use the *Guide* as a bookmark; by keeping the *Guide* nearby and occasionally reviewing the *Guide Words* you will still receive the *Guide's* many benefits.

affirm page 42

Use simple one-line affirmations (positive statements worded in the present) throughout the day, especially when you need a quick pep talk. *Affirm* to reduce stress and to put yourself in a positive frame of mind. For example, "I read quickly and comprehend fully in a relaxed manner."

aim page 29

When actions have no clear purpose, they're seldom carried out effectively. To concentrate on your reading or any activity you need both a tangible purpose and an expected outcome. Your mind needs clues to *aim* toward a goal, and it needs incentives to stay on that goal. When your mind identifies a purpose, it will instinctively grasp what is important and skim over the rest. Ask the *Guiding Question: Why am I reading this?* all the time, especially before you commit yourself to a new book and whenever you find your mind wandering as you read. Repeat the *Guiding Question* until it is a habit, and you will begin to trust your subconscious to seize the essential and reject the unimportant.

break page 46

Take short *breaks* every 30 to 60 minutes. Breaks energize and relax; many breaks have a lesson to teach; memory is greater before and after breaks. Try deep breathing, visualizing, palming, exercising, stretching, light reading, and updating your schedule for tomorrow. Break before burnout.

breathe page 39

The more difficult the activity, the more important it is to regulate your *breathing*. Regulate your breathing by taking long, deep belly breaths. Contract your diaphragm as you exhale, expand your diaphragm as you inhale. Combine it with your moment of affirmation and visualization.

concentrate page 24

Always *concentrate* on the task at hand. Think of nothing but your reading; let all stray thoughts pass easily like clouds drifting overhead. Improve concentration by always reading with a purpose (ask the *Guiding Question: Why am I reading this*?). Concentrate on moving your eyes forward; regression and backskipping are bad habits. When you increase your reading speed you prevent your mind from wandering, thereby increasing concentration. Practice reading in a noisy spot to improve concentration.

experiment page 54

The more creative leeway you have in developing a personal style for doing things, the more you will benefit. Different types of reading material should be read in different ways. Develop an arsenal of techniques that will handle different situations—***experiment*** with different methods and choose what works best. Many suggestions are given in Chapter 12.

flow page 21

Performance is best when action and thought are smooth, steady and continuous; develop a rhythm. When reading, let your mind and eyes ***flow*** over the text with the aid of the *Guide*. This will engage your peripheral vision. By increasing the amount seen with each fixation of the eye, comprehension will improve because words have more meaning when viewed together. A soft focus will also increase your peripheral vision. Focus softly at the text by relaxing your eye muscles and gazing at the text. As a variation on this, let your eyes follow the white space just above the line of text (a good technique to try when not using a visual guide). The faster you read, the softer the focus of your eyes.

map page 48

Take notes to reinforce ideas in your memory. Use a key word or two to represent the broad concepts. Put the ideas into two-dimensional mind ***maps***. Make them visual and creative; include color, pictures and diagrams. Take notes that are worth remembering. Highlight or underline text and summarize ideas in the margins when appropriate.

persist page 59

Learn to work unceasingly and tenaciously toward your goal. Adopt an emphatic and resolute attitude that will guide you through any undertaking. ***Persist*** in practicing and using the skills presented in this book—the only way to learn and understand these techniques and to turn them into habits. Start by making a commitment to read this book over many times during the next few weeks and months.

plan page 52

Prioritize all your activities, including various types of reading (e.g., work-related, newspapers, pleasure). Keep a written schedule, block out time to read, then do it. *Plan* how to read each item before you begin (a part of preview, Chapter 5). Always carry a book for those unexpected periods of free time.

practice page 24

Practice is the best way to learn, understand and remember a new skill; it is the only way to turn something into a habit. Always **remember to use the Guide** when you read. By practicing your reading with the *Guide* you will have a constant reminder to push yourself to use the techniques you've learned; it's like yarn tied around your finger. Practice will make speed reading comfortable and automatic. The motivation to practice must come from within. Understanding this will come through practice: the more you practice, the more you will achieve; the more you achieve, the more you will be motivated. Practice makes progress.

preview page 28

Preview to get an overview and feel for an activity before you begin; it helps identify a purpose (see also "aim") and lets you know what to expect. Previewing engages your brain and prepares it for action—or inaction, if you decide a book or activity is inappropriate. Previewing also helps to create an interest—important when faced with boring material. Read the cover and the before and after material to see what's there for you. *Flip* through the pages to get a feel for the layout; stop and do some sample reading if anything catches your eye. *Hyperscan* the book or the parts you expect to read by making rapid (3 to 7 seconds per page) sweeps with your *Guide* over every page. Relax and don't try to remember what you see, but feel yourself comprehending the material. Keep a soft focus (see Chapter 3) and take in the big picture. Finally, *choose your strategy*. Do not treat every book in the same way (i.e., word-by-word, page-by-page). You've identified what you need to know, now identify the best way to get it (suggestions in Chapters 6 and 12); remember, a decision not to read something is acceptable.

relax page 37

A ***relaxed*** person performs better; too much tension and stress reduces your ability to learn. Choose comfortable surroundings, choose a comfortable seat, take a few deep breaths, and go through the rituals necessary to concentrate on the task at hand.

remember page 44

Improve your memory to perform better. We ***remember*** things that are meaningful and interesting. Make it interesting by previewing (Chapter 5). Test your comprehension by asking: What did I just learn? Concentrate on your purpose (ask the *Guiding Question:* ***Why am I reading this***?) and attempt to remember only the relevant material. Use repetition: think about the material after you read it, take notes, talk about it, read it a second time. Take breaks—memory is greater at the beginning and end of a learning session. *Keep in mind that even if you read a book slowly, you remember only a fraction of the information—the same amount as you would if you read it through quickly—unless you reinforce the memory.*

sense page 35

Let your feelings evaluate your actions to instinctively adjust to a changing environment—be flexible. Let your subconscious ***sense*** the reading material and automatically vary your speed and technique as the difficulty, importance and redundancy of the material changes—a state of mind that lets you read "on a roll." Let your intuition and peripheral vision work to grab what is important from the changing terrain of words and ideas. The more flexibility you develop in your reading, the more you will trust your subconscious.

visualize page 41

Discipline your daydreaming for positive results. Great achievements occur by first creating a mental picture of fulfilling a goal and then focusing energy on that *visualization*, allowing it to happen. See and feel yourself as a reading master. Combine visualization with breathing and palming (page 47).

Getting Started with the Guide Words

By first learning to use the *Guide Words* to read intelligently, you develop both an understanding of them and the habit of using them. You're now prepared to use them in any situation to help you learn and achieve top performance.

Look at them often whenever you start something new, go astray from the activity at hand, get stuck on a problem or are faced with a difficult task. From starting a new job to taking a test, even to becoming a better skier, the *Guide Words* can help.

You can use the *Guide Words* in various ways. At the simplest level, just take a 3-minute break from your activity and read down the list of words. Think about the activity or problem as it relates to each word. As thoughts surface, make note of the two or three best ideas that will get you going again. Turn them into affirmations if appropriate. Then act on them. Repeat this process whenever necessary.

To apply the *Guide Words* at the highest level, draw a mind map, introduced in Chapter 10 (page 48). A mind map of your project or activity becomes a written plan for reaching your goal. A mind map with the *Guide Words* helps you become aware of the whole-brain process necessary for achieving top performance.

This patterning is a brainstorming process so all ideas are welcome, regardless of their absurdity; but don't get bogged down in detail. Do it quickly, then add to it later. Print with as few words as possible, turning the paper if necessary. Be sure to connect words or ideas between branches that are related. Be creative and experiment. If necessary, start over and adjust the size of your writing or the size of your paper. Do a mind map for the present situation, planning to do it over in the future if circumstances change.

Remember: the *Guide Words* aren't rules, only *guidelines*. This is not a rigid system; not all *Guide Words* work well in every application. Experiment then add, stretch, delete, modify and expand upon the words to suit your style and the specific activity. The *Guide Words* are all interrelated.

Example: The Guide Words for Time Management

Following are some general notes we made for applying the *Guide Words* to the art of time management. We've presented them in text because mind maps by someone else are confusing; however, we've started our mind map for one of the words as a comparison. How would you finish it?

1) *Affirm*—Say to yourself, "I manage myself superbly, always achieving my goals."
2) *Aim*—To achieve a goal, ask yourself, "What am I trying to accomplish?" followed by "Lakein's Question: What is the best use of my time now?"
3) *Break*—Schedule breaks in your daily schedule, as well as plan what to accomplish during those breaks.
4) *Breathe*—Use this technique with visualizations and affirmations. Use deep breathing to stay centered, boost energy, improve concentration, and handle unforeseen stressful events.
5) *Concentration*—Concentrate fully on the task at hand. Avoid doing too many activities at once. Manage a large project by breaking it into smaller tasks.
6) *Experiment*—Experiment with new time management techniques; schedule time to try them. Develop your personal style for managing time.
7) *Flow*—Proceed steadily and continuously through your daily activities. Be aware of your environment and adapt to changing conditions. When bogged down in detail, expand your focus to see the issue in context.
8) *Map*—Always keep a written schedule for the day nearby. Take notes to document progress and important

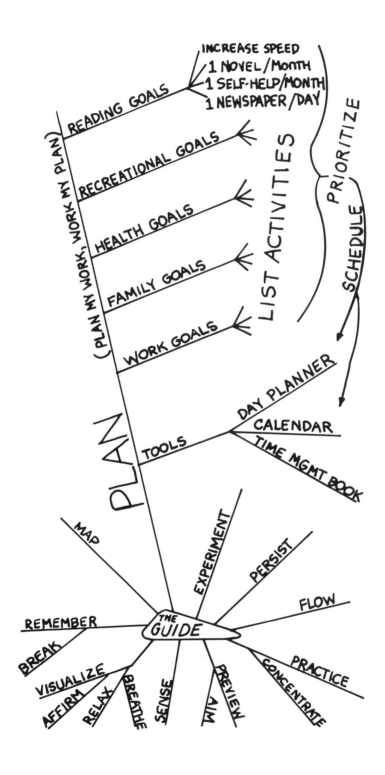

information. Use mind maps to break up and analyze large projects.

9) *Persist*—Persist through all obstacles and mistakes to manage your time well and achieve what you set out to accomplish.

10) *Plan*—Planning is what time management is all about. Set goals and assign priorities to the activities necessary to achieve those goals. Acquire the tools and materials necessary to manage your time: a day-planner, a calendar, and probably a book or manual on time management. Plan your work, work your plan.

11) *Practice*—Consciously practice the components of time management until they become a natural process. Practice asking "Lakein's Question: What is the best use of my time now?" until it is a habit.

12) *Preview*—Look at the big picture; get an overview and feel for your day. Pick a purpose and strategy, as well as identify potential problems. Become aware of your time-use habits so you can change unproductive patterns.

13) *Relax*—Use all relaxation techniques. A calm and centered person makes better decisions and better use of her or his time.

14) *Remember*—Review your goals and remember your priorities. Reinforce important information that you need to remember.

15) *Sense*—Don't hold blindly to something. Once you've committed yourself to an activity, pay attention to your feelings. They may signal you to change your priority, strategy or activity. Be flexible.

16) *Visualize*—See yourself organized and relaxed, having accomplished your daily "To Do" list with time left over for fun. Picture and feel yourself as a master of the art of time management.

One final point. The *Guide Words* can be used both to help you *perform* an activity and to help you *learn* an activity. The steps above describe the *performance* of time management and not the *learning* of time management. To see the difference, compare the use of the word *preview* above with the following use of *preview* as it relates to learning time management:

Preview—Go to a library or bookstore and browse four or five books on time management; call your local community college, ask what courses they offer on time management, then call the instructors for information; and talk with busy people who manage their time well.

By using the *Guide Words* you'll be taking a big step away from traditional learning methods—and a huge leap toward becoming a whole-brain performer. The more you use this model, the more natural it will become. Keep an open and fluid mind and reach for the top. Start now.

Meet the Talent

ROSE SAPERSTEIN has been described by her colleagues as faster than a speeding eyeball, more powerful than the information explosion and able to skim tall books in a single stare. She developed this ability during five years as an instructor for the Institute for Reading Education and Development in Seattle. Now a learning consultant, she consults and gives seminars on speed reading, learning skills, time management and creativity, and is a seminar administrator in management, selling and customer relations for Learning International (a Times Mirror Company). She has taught at Antioch University Seattle and for the University of Washington. Ms. Saperstein is on the board of directors for New Horizons for Learning, an information network for progressive education that sponsors a yearly international conference on current learning trends.

JAMES JOSEPH is a former student of Ms. Saperstein and a reformed nonreader—he could read but chose not to. He is now an author and book producer.

DOUG KEITH is an award-winning illustrator whose books include the *Elfabet* and *Kreplachness Monster*. He owns a design studio where he does work in advertising and TV and has won a regional Emmy for graphic design.

Suggestion Box

Read Your Way to the Top is the first in our innovative series of business self-help books. We hope this book has been helpful and inspiring, and has made learning fun. We welcome your comments and suggestions.

The Publisher

Speedy Order Blank

Please ask for *Read Your Way to the Top with the Guide* at your local bookstore. If you can't find it there, we'll be glad to fill your order.

_____ book(s) and *Guide(s)*, $7.95 plus
     $1.00 postage $8.95 $ _____

_____ extra *Guide(s)*, $1.00 plus $.25 postage $1.25 $ _____

_____ 7.9% tax because you live in Washington $ _____

Please include check or money order.   Total $ _____

This book may be deductible under I.R.C. Section 162. Please discuss this with your tax advisor.

Name _____

Address _____

City/State/Zip _____

Please **PHOTOCOPY** this form and return to:
     Bluechip Publishers
     Attn: Sally Freeman
     P.O. Box 31236
     Seattle, WA 98103

Are you thinking about using *Read Your Way to the Top* as a training aid or gift for members of your organization? If so, please request info on quantity discounts, including imprinting your organization's name on the *Guide* and customized mailing envelopes. Are you thinking about lectures and seminars for your business? Just ask and we'll fill you in on the details.